FREEDOM'S PROMISE

TWO
BLOODY SUNDAYS
CIVIL RIGHTS IN AMERICA AND IRELAND

BY DUCHESS HARRIS, JD, PHD

Cover image: Civil rights activist Amelia Boynton is helped up
after police attacked demonstrators in Selma, Alabama.

Title page image: People march in memory of those killed
during the events of Bloody Sunday in Ireland.

Core Library

An Imprint of Abdo Publishing
abdobooks.com

abdocorelibrary.com

Published by Abdo Publishing, a division of ABDO, PO Box 398166,
Minneapolis, Minnesota 55439. Copyright © 2019 by Abdo Consulting
Group, Inc. International copyrights reserved in all countries. No part of this
book may be reproduced in any form without written permission from the
publisher. Core Library™ is a trademark and logo of Abdo Publishing.

Printed in the United States of America, North Mankato, Minnesota
092018
012019

Cover Photo: Charles Moore/Premium Archive/Getty Images
Interior Photos: Edward Kitch/AP Images, 1; Bill Frakes/AP Images, 5; Charles Moore/
Premium Archive/Getty Images, 6–7; AP Images, 8–9; Popperfoto/Getty Images, 12; Atlanta
Journal-Constitution/AP Images, 16–17, 43; Warren K. Leffler/Everett Collection/Newscom, 19;
Red Line Editorial, 21, 38; Leif Skoogfors/Corbis Historical/Getty Images, 26–27; Peter Kemp/AP
Images, 29; Central Press/Hulton Archive/Getty Images, 32–33; Brian Little/PAMPC PA/AP Images,
36–37

Editor: Maddie Spalding
Series Designer: Claire Vanden Branden
Contributor: Martha London

Library of Congress Control Number: 2018949701

Publisher's Cataloging-in-Publication Data

Names: Harris, Duchess, author.
Title: Two bloody Sundays: civil rights in America and Ireland / by Duchess Harris
Other title: Civil rights in America and Ireland
Description: Minneapolis, Minnesota : Abdo Publishing, 2019 | Series: Freedom's
    promise | Includes online resources and index.
Identifiers: ISBN 9781532117770 (lib. bdg.) | ISBN 9781641856119 (pbk) | ISBN
    9781532170638 (ebook)
Subjects: LCSH: Bloody Sunday, Derry, Northern Ireland, 1972--Juvenile
    literature. | Selma to Montgomery Rights March (1965 : Selma, Ala.)--Juvenile
    literature. | Civil rights movements--Juvenile literature. | Civil rights
    demonstrations--Juvenile literature.
Classification: DDC 323.1196073076--dc23

CONTENTS

A LETTER FROM DUCHESS

In 1965 African Americans in Selma, Alabama, marched for the right to vote. In 1972 Catholics in Derry, Northern Ireland, marched against injustice in their own nation. Both peaceful protests ended in violence, and the events in both places became known as Bloody Sunday.

On the surface, you might not be able to imagine what Derry and Selma had in common, but the Catholics in Ireland saw similarities in their struggles. They felt a connection with black Americans in the southern United States. Both groups were fighting for their civil rights.

Throughout history, the struggle for civil rights has not been limited to one time or place. These movements have influenced each other in important ways.

Please join me in learning about Selma's impact on Northern Ireland. Join me in a journey that tells the story of the promise of freedom.

Duchess Harris

President Barack Obama spoke at the site of the Bloody Sunday in Selma, Alabama, on the fiftieth anniversary of the event.

CHAPTER
ONE

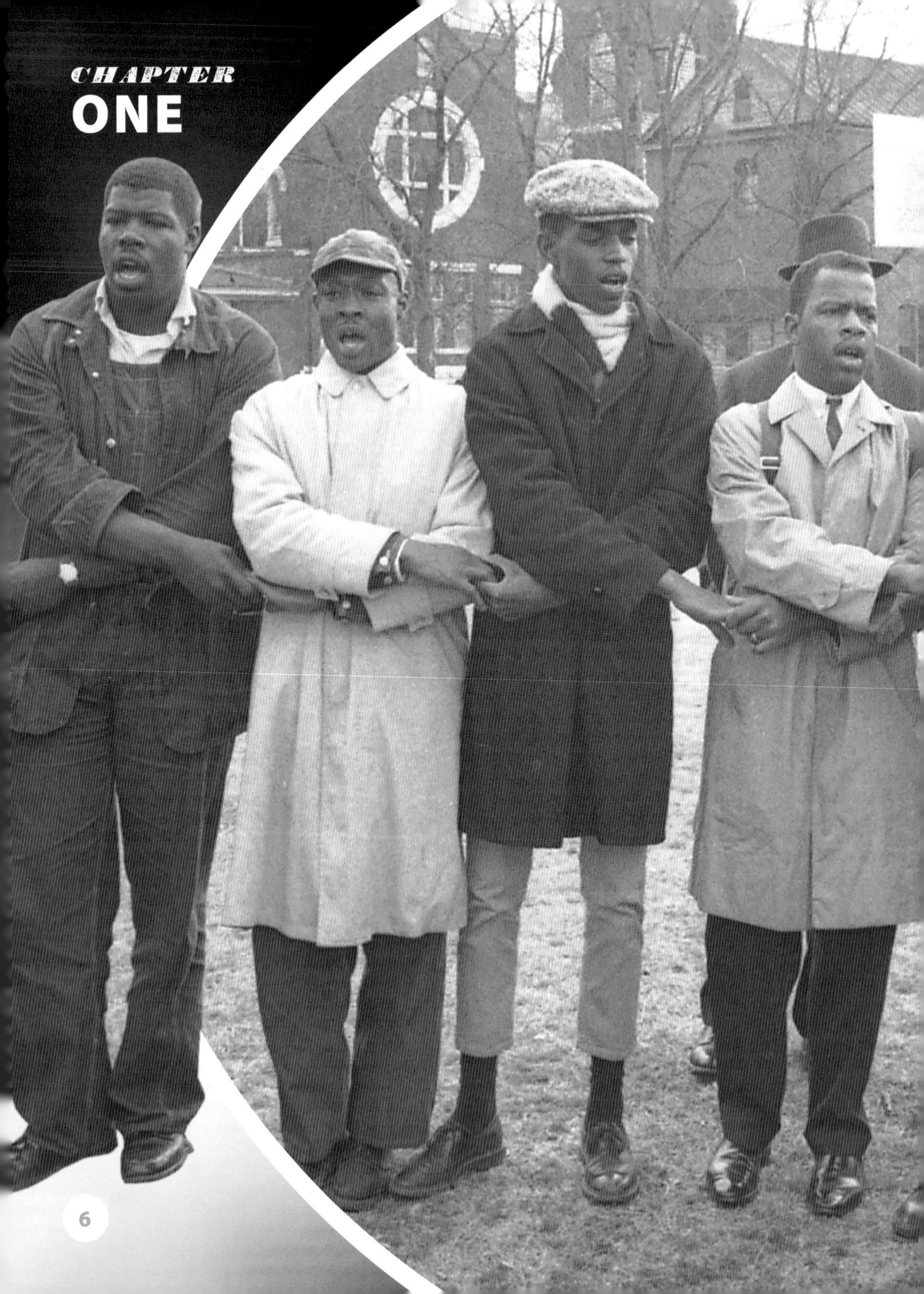

BLOODY SUNDAYS

The morning of March 7, 1965, was cool and crisp. It was a good day for a march. Six hundred black protesters gathered outside Brown Chapel African Methodist Episcopal Church in Selma, Alabama. The protesters were ready to walk the 54 miles (87 km) to Alabama's state capital, Montgomery. They were protesting barriers that kept them from voting. In the South, African Americans were often forced to take literacy tests or pay a poll tax in order to vote. The protesters hoped their march would change this.

Activists including John Lewis, *second from right*, held hands and sang protest songs before the attempted march in Selma, Alabama.

Officers sprayed tear gas at marchers as they tried to cross the Edmund Pettus Bridge in Selma.

Alabama's governor told the protesters that they could not march. He sent police officers and state troopers to Selma. The police were supposed to make sure the protesters did not leave the city. The protesters were prepared to make the journey anyway.

The Edmund Pettus Bridge was six blocks away from the church. The bridge was on the road

to Montgomery. The protesters had to cross the bridge. But police officers stood in their way. White families stood alongside the road. They yelled at the protesters.

The protesters faced the white officers. They were at a standstill. The protesters could not continue forward. The sheriff told them to turn around. The protesters ignored him. They tried to walk forward in a single-file line. But they were blocked. Officers started walking toward the protesters. The officers put on gas masks. They threw tear gas at the protesters. Tear gas causes breathing difficulties and temporary blindness. The officers hit the protesters with heavy wooden clubs. The crowd of white onlookers cheered. The officers then chased the protesters back to the church where the march had begun. At the end of the day, more than 50 protesters were injured.

Television crews filmed the whole event. The assault on the bridge was televised that night across the United States. The media coverage turned the incident into a national civil rights issue. The Selma protest changed the course of the American civil rights movement. This event would become known as Bloody Sunday.

NORTHERN IRELAND

Seven years after the Selma Bloody Sunday, a different Bloody Sunday occurred in Northern Ireland. On January 30, 1972, 10,000 Catholic protesters gathered in Derry, Northern Ireland. They were protesting mistreatment by British troops. British soldiers had arrested people they suspected were part of a Catholic resistance group called the Irish Republican Army (IRA). The soldiers held these suspects without trial.

The protesters started to march toward Derry's city center. But soldiers from the British army had set up roadblocks. The roadblocks prevented protesters from reaching their destination.

British soldiers confronted protesters in Derry, Northern Ireland, on January 30, 1972.

Some protesters threw rocks at the soldiers. Soldiers responded with violence. They used a water cannon to hose protesters. They also released tear gas into the crowd. Soldiers were posted in buildings throughout the city. They had powerful guns. Some of these soldiers shot into the crowd. They injured two men.

The protesters continued to march toward the soldiers. The soldiers did not move. The British government had told the soldiers to arrest people. But some decided to fire their guns instead. Within minutes, they had shot 26 protesters. Thirteen of them died on the street. Another protester was severely injured. He died from his injuries a few months later.

The citizens of Northern Ireland saw this as murder. British leaders said the crowd shot at the soldiers first. But none of the protesters had been armed.

Bloody Sunday in Northern Ireland received a lot of attention. Many people in Northern Ireland wanted to be free of English rule. They also wanted justice for the people who had been shot.

NONVIOLENT PROTEST

Throughout history, governments or groups in power have oppressed certain people. In the 1960s, white people denied African Americans their rights. Many African Americans joined the American civil rights movement. They fought for equal rights. In the 1970s, Protestant leaders mistreated Catholics in Northern

Ireland. The British government supported Protestant leaders. Irish Catholics who fought for their rights were part of the Northern Ireland civil rights movement. They were inspired by civil rights protests in the United States.

GANDHI'S INFLUENCE

Mahatma Gandhi was an activist in India in the early 1900s. He protested against British rule in India. The British mistreated the Indian people. Gandhi used nonviolent strategies to make changes in his country. He organized mass protests, including boycotts of British goods. Martin Luther King Jr. was influenced by Gandhi. King traveled in India in 1959. He met with the Gandhi family. He believed Gandhi's method was the only way people could successfully fight for their freedom.

Activists have to choose how to protest. Some activists protest violently. Others use nonviolent protest. African American activist Martin Luther King Jr. advocated for nonviolent protest. So did many other American civil rights leaders. They believed violence would not help them achieve equality.

Nonviolent protests included marches to state capitals. Some black protesters organized sit-ins. They went into restaurants where black people were not welcome. Protesters often faced physical and verbal attacks. But they did not fight back with violence.

The Selma march was a type of nonviolent protest. The march in Derry was also meant to be nonviolent. Although some marchers later decided to throw rocks, all were unarmed. Most had hoped to bring about change peacefully.

EXPLORE ONLINE

Chapter One talks about nonviolent protest. This type of protest has played an important role in many civil rights movements. The article at the website below goes into more depth on this topic. How is the information from the website the same as the information in Chapter One? What new information did you learn from the website?

MARTIN LUTHER KING JR. AND NONVIOLENT PROTEST
abdocorelibrary.com/two-bloody-sundays

CHAPTER
TWO

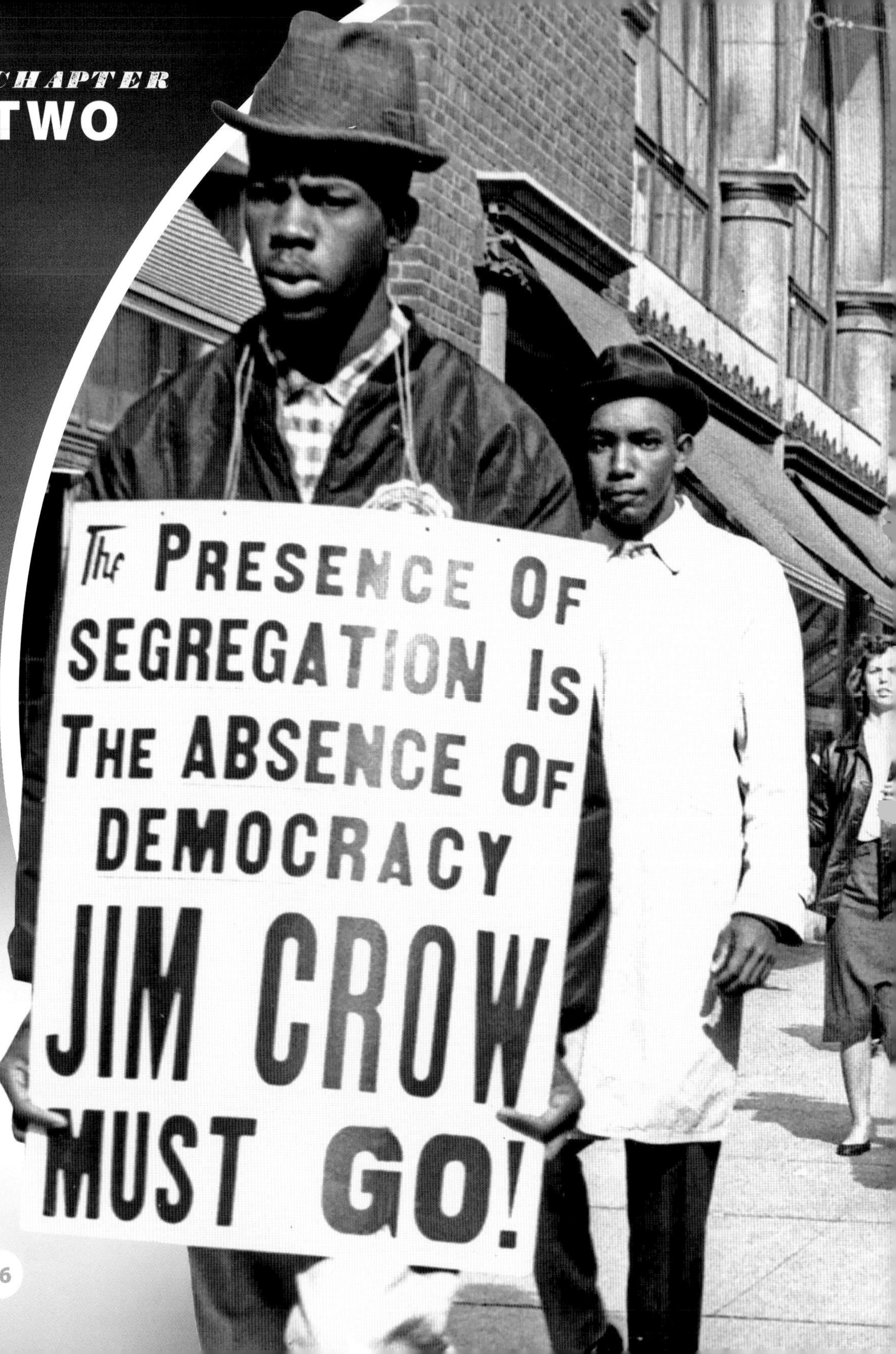
The PRESENCE OF
SEGREGATION IS
THE ABSENCE OF
DEMOCRACY
JIM CROW
MUST GO!

CIVIL RIGHTS IN THE UNITED STATES

The voting obstacles that people protested in Selma were part of a larger problem in the South. Enslaved black people were freed after the American Civil War (1861–1865). But white people in the South had wanted to keep their power over the freed black people. They enacted laws that discriminated against African Americans. These laws were called Jim Crow laws. Jim Crow laws enforced racial segregation, or the separation of people into groups based on the color of their skin. This practice was designed

African American marchers protested segregation at a department store in Atlanta, Georgia, in 1961.

to keep black and white people from interacting. Black people could not use the same services as white people. Separate entrances to restaurants were created for black people. White and black people even used different water fountains.

In 1896 the US Supreme Court ruled that segregation was legal in a case called *Plessy v. Ferguson*. The court said that the separate but equal rule was fair. The separate but equal rule said that as long as the same services were offered to black and white people, it did not matter whether they were separated from each other.

The separate but equal rule was not reversed until 1954. In that year, the Supreme Court ruled in a case called *Brown v. Board of Education of Topeka*. This ruling said that schools across the United States had to be integrated. Black students had to be allowed to attend the same schools as white students.

Schools began integrating after the *Brown v. Board of Education* decision.

VOTER REGISTRATION

The Fifteenth Amendment to the US Constitution guaranteed African American men the right to vote. The amendment was passed into law in 1870. But local governments in the South created obstacles to keep black people from voting. Black people often had to pass literacy tests in order to vote. These tests were supposed to prove an understanding of the Constitution. But the tests were difficult and confusing. Even well-educated people could not pass these tests. Southern states also used poll taxes to keep black people from voting. African Americans who could not pay the tax were not allowed to register to vote. Another obstacle that some states used was called the grandfather clause. The grandfather clause allowed people to vote only if their ancestors had voted. Most African Americans' ancestors had not been able to vote. So they also were not allowed to vote.

The Civil Rights Act was passed in 1964. This law made it illegal to discriminate against people based on their race. But states continued to create obstacles that kept black people from voting. Civil rights groups fought against this injustice. The Student Nonviolent Coordinating Committee (SNCC) worked to register black people to vote in the South. This was not easy. Many black people were frightened to register. Members of the Ku Klux Klan (KKK) beat and murdered black people in the South. The KKK is an all-white organization. It believes white people are superior to black people. The KKK and other racist white people sometimes threatened black people who tried to vote.

THE CIVIL RIGHTS ACT OF 1964

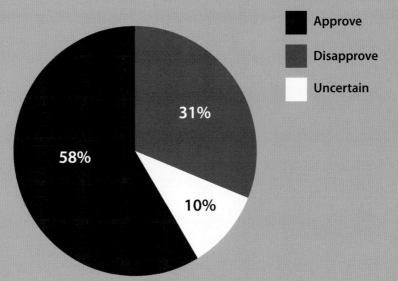

Approve

Disapprove

Uncertain

31%

58%

10%

The above graph shows the results of a poll taken of a sample of Americans in October 1964, shortly after the passing of the Civil Rights Act. The graph shows the percentage of people who agreed or disagreed with the law as well as those who were not certain. (Due to rounding, the percentages do not add up to 100 percent.) What does this graph tell you about civil rights support in the country at the time?

BEFORE THE MARCH

About a month before the Selma Bloody Sunday, a black man named Jimmie Lee Jackson was killed. Jackson had been participating in a voting rights march in Marion, Alabama. Police officers attacked his mother. Jackson tried to protect her. The officers shot and killed Jackson. This violence prompted King to come to Selma. He helped plan a march from Selma to Montgomery.

News outlets often did not cover civil rights events. This lack of coverage frustrated King. He told *Life* magazine about the upcoming march. He hoped this would draw media attention to the march. His plan worked.

MARCHING FOR CIVIL RIGHTS

In the aftermath of the Selma Bloody Sunday, the church where the march had begun turned into an emergency hospital. Police stayed outside the church for hours. They did not allow activists to move the injured people out of the church. When the police finally left, more than 50 people were sent to the local hospital.

The police attack on the Edmund Pettus Bridge was filmed. That night, the film coverage was aired on national television. It interrupted a movie about World War II (1941–1945). The movie talked about the

Holocaust and the crimes the Nazis had committed. The Nazis had oppressed and killed Jewish people. Americans saw similarities between the Nazis' treatment of Jewish people and the brutality of the police in Selma. The broadcast of the event caused public outrage.

Two days later, King led another march to the bridge. Police and state troopers again blocked the bridge. The Alabama governor did not want the protesters to walk to Montgomery.

PERSPECTIVES

LYNDON B. JOHNSON

President Lyndon B. Johnson gave a speech to the US Congress one week after Bloody Sunday. Johnson had created a bill to remove the barriers that kept black people from voting. He urged Congress to support his bill. He talked about the events of Bloody Sunday. He argued that no citizens should be denied their rights. He said: "We are met here tonight as Americans—not as Democrats or Republicans—we are met here as Americans to solve that problem."

On March 21, 1965, a march to Montgomery began again. This time the marchers successfully crossed the bridge. President Lyndon B. Johnson had called in National Guard troops to protect the marchers. Approximately 3,200 people joined King on the journey. The march took five days. The marchers walked 12 miles (19 km) each day and slept in fields. When they reached Montgomery, the crowd had grown to 25,000 people. They gathered in front of the state capitol building. King and other activists spoke to the crowd. They delivered messages of hope for a peaceful future.

THE EDMUND PETTUS BRIDGE

The Edmund Pettus Bridge was named after a Confederate general in the American Civil War. Edmund Pettus was also an Alabama state senator and a KKK leader. He died in 1907. The bridge was named after him 40 years later. It still stands today. Its name has not been changed.

STRAIGHT TO THE
SOURCE

Activist John Lewis was one of the leaders of the Selma march. He later became a US representative for the state of Georgia. In a 2015 interview, Lewis explained the importance of the march:

> In Selma, Alabama, in 1965, only 2.1 percent of blacks of voting age were registered to vote. The only place you could attempt to register was to go down to the courthouse. You had to pass a so-called literacy test. . . . On one occasion, a man was asked to count the number of bubbles on a bar of soap. On another occasion, a man was asked to count the number of jellybeans in a jar. There were African-American lawyers, doctors, teachers, housewives, college professors flunking this so-called literacy test.

> Source: "'I Thought I Saw Death': John Lewis Remembers Police Attack on Bloody Sunday in Selma 50 Years Ago." *Democracy Now*. Democracy Now, March 6, 2015. Web. Accessed July 6, 2018.

Back It Up

The author of this passage is using evidence to support a point. Write a paragraph describing the point the author is making. Then write down two or three pieces of evidence the author uses to make the point.

CHAPTER THREE

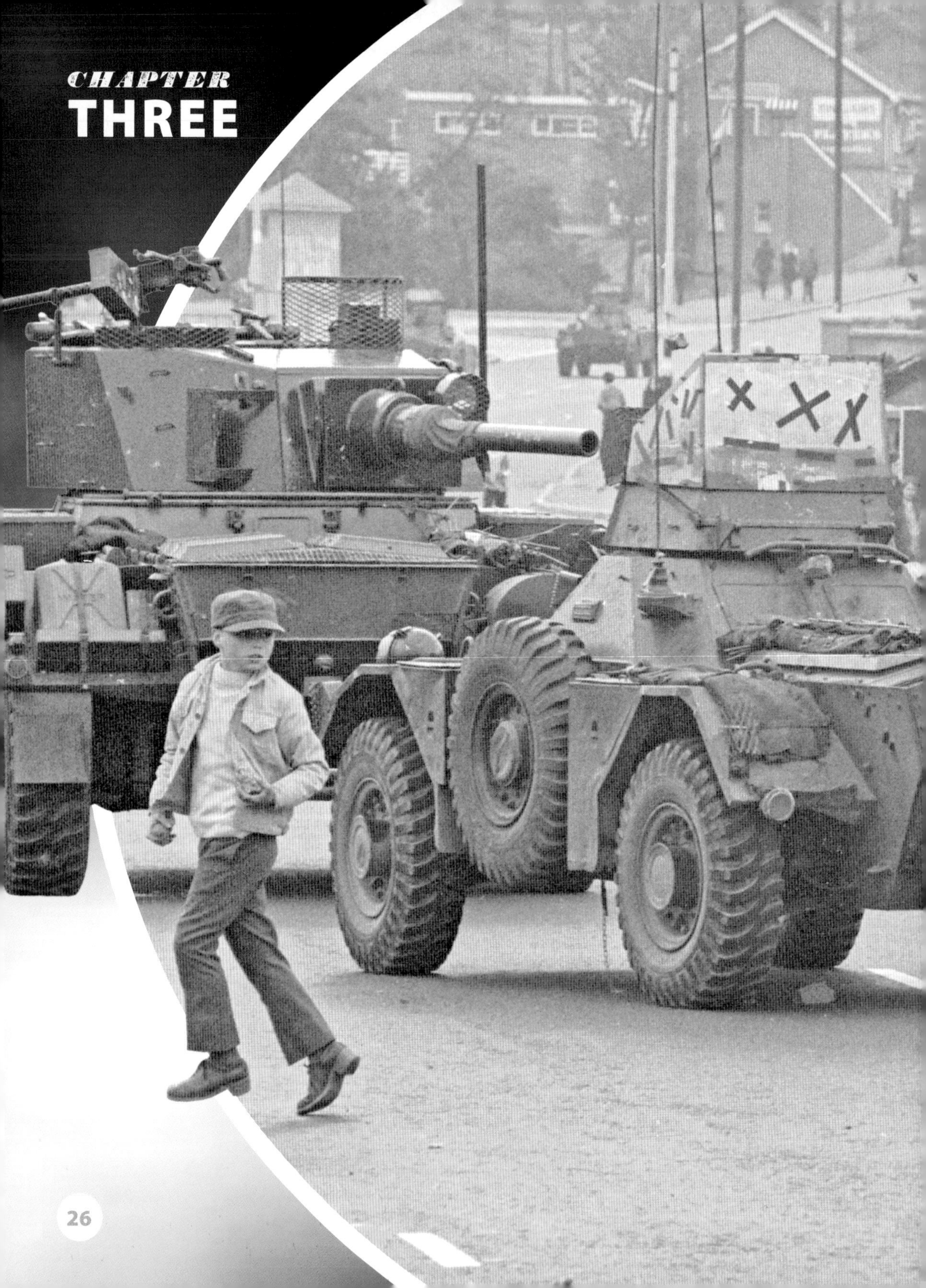

CIVIL RIGHTS IN NORTHERN IRELAND

Decades of conflict and unrest preceded Bloody Sunday in Northern Ireland. In May 1921, Ireland split into Northern Ireland and the Republic of Ireland. Six counties in the north became Northern Ireland. Northern Ireland remained part of the United Kingdom. Twenty-six counties in the south became the Republic of Ireland. The Republic became an independent state. Northern Ireland was mostly occupied by Protestants. But Catholics lived in Northern Ireland as well. Protestants and Catholics

British tanks came in to patrol the streets of Northern Ireland in the late 1960s.

are both part of the Christian church. They have similar beliefs. But social and cultural differences created disagreements between the two groups. Most Protestants supported British rule. They wanted Northern Ireland to remain in the United Kingdom. They called themselves Unionists. Many Catholics wanted to be independent from the United Kingdom. They called themselves Nationalists.

In the 1960s, Catholics in Northern Ireland fought for their civil rights. Protestants had been mistreating Catholics for decades. Catholics had a hard time finding jobs and homes. Protestant employers often chose to hire other Protestants. Protestants often chose to rent or sell homes to other Protestants. Voting laws made these issues hard to fix. Only people who owned houses could vote in elections. Citizens who rented homes were not allowed to vote. Many Catholics did not own houses. They were unable to vote.

Activists marched in London, England, to protest voting restrictions in Northern Ireland.

CIVIL RIGHTS GROUPS

In 1967 the Northern Ireland Civil Rights Association (NICRA) was formed. NICRA protested voting discrimination. The organization argued that all citizens should be able to vote. NICRA members believed that property ownership should not be a voting requirement.

They thought that if they could get Catholic citizens to the polls, political change would follow. Another civil rights group called the **Derry Housing Action Committee (DHAC)** formed in 1968. The group was founded in the city of Derry. The DHAC protested against housing discrimination.

Many Irish civil rights leaders took notes from African American activists. Protesters saw similarities between the treatment of African Americans and Irish Catholics. African Americans sometimes called themselves "negroes." This term is widely considered offensive today. But it was commonly used in the 1960s.

BERNADETTE DEVLIN

Bernadette Devlin was an activist in Northern Ireland in the 1960s and 1970s. She witnessed the events of Bloody Sunday. Devlin later helped found a political party called the People's Democracy. The People's Democracy focuses on civil rights. Devlin also founded the Irish Republican Socialist Party. She dedicated her career to social justice work.

Some Catholics in Northern Ireland began to call themselves "white negroes." They sang "We Shall Overcome" at meetings and marches. This song had been an anthem for black people during the American civil rights movement. Some Irish leaders even went to the United States. They met with American activists. These meetings helped them plan their own protests.

Activists in Northern Ireland watched television coverage of the American civil rights movement. They learned about the Selma Bloody Sunday. This inspired a march in Northern Ireland. Activists marched from Belfast to Derry in Northern Ireland in early 1969. They marched for equal rights. Activists also organized sit-downs. These protests were similar to sit-ins. A large group of activists would sit down in a public area. Groups such as the DHAC sometimes organized them. The DHAC held a sit-down in July 1968. DHAC members sat on a bridge in Derry. They did this to bring attention to housing discrimination.

Some more extreme members of the IRA bombed public places to protest British rule in Northern Ireland.

One of the most well-known Catholic resistance groups was the IRA. This group protested and rioted against British rule. Protestant leaders tried to squash the growing independence movement. They used force against Catholics.

British leaders sent military troops into Northern Ireland. The troops were instructed to arrest IRA members. But troops did not arrest only IRA members.

They arrested anyone they thought was part of the
IRA. These prisoners were held without trial. Hundreds
of Catholics came together on Sunday, January 30,
1972, to protest this injustice. They gathered for a
march in Derry. They linked arms. They sang "We Shall
Overcome" as they marched. The event turned violent
when British soldiers shot at the crowd. Bloody Sunday
would have a long-lasting effect on Northern Ireland.

THE AFTERMATH

In the week after Bloody Sunday, the British prime minister appointed Lord John Passmore Widgery to investigate the incident. Widgery was an English judge. Many people in Ireland doubted he would do a good job.

Widgery's investigation did not take long. He published his findings on April 18, 1972. The Widgery report found the British army innocent. It concluded that the British soldiers acted in self-defense. Widgery said that the Irish protesters shot first. There was no evidence to support this claim.

Widgery's report made people in Northern Ireland angrier. Many people believe that Bloody Sunday and Widgery's report made the Northern Ireland conflict last much longer than it otherwise would have. In April 1998, British and Irish government officials signed the Good Friday Agreement. This agreement finally ended the conflict. It created a new government in Northern Ireland. The new government was made up of both Unionists and Nationalists. This cooperation helped create a new era of peace in Northern Ireland.

FURTHER EVIDENCE

Chapter Three discusses the causes and effects of Bloody Sunday in Northern Ireland. What was one of the main points of this chapter? What evidence is included to support this point? Read the article at the website below. Does the information on the website support this point? Or does it present new evidence?

BLOODY SUNDAY IN NORTHERN IRELAND
abdocorelibrary.com/two-bloody-sundays

CHAPTER
FOUR

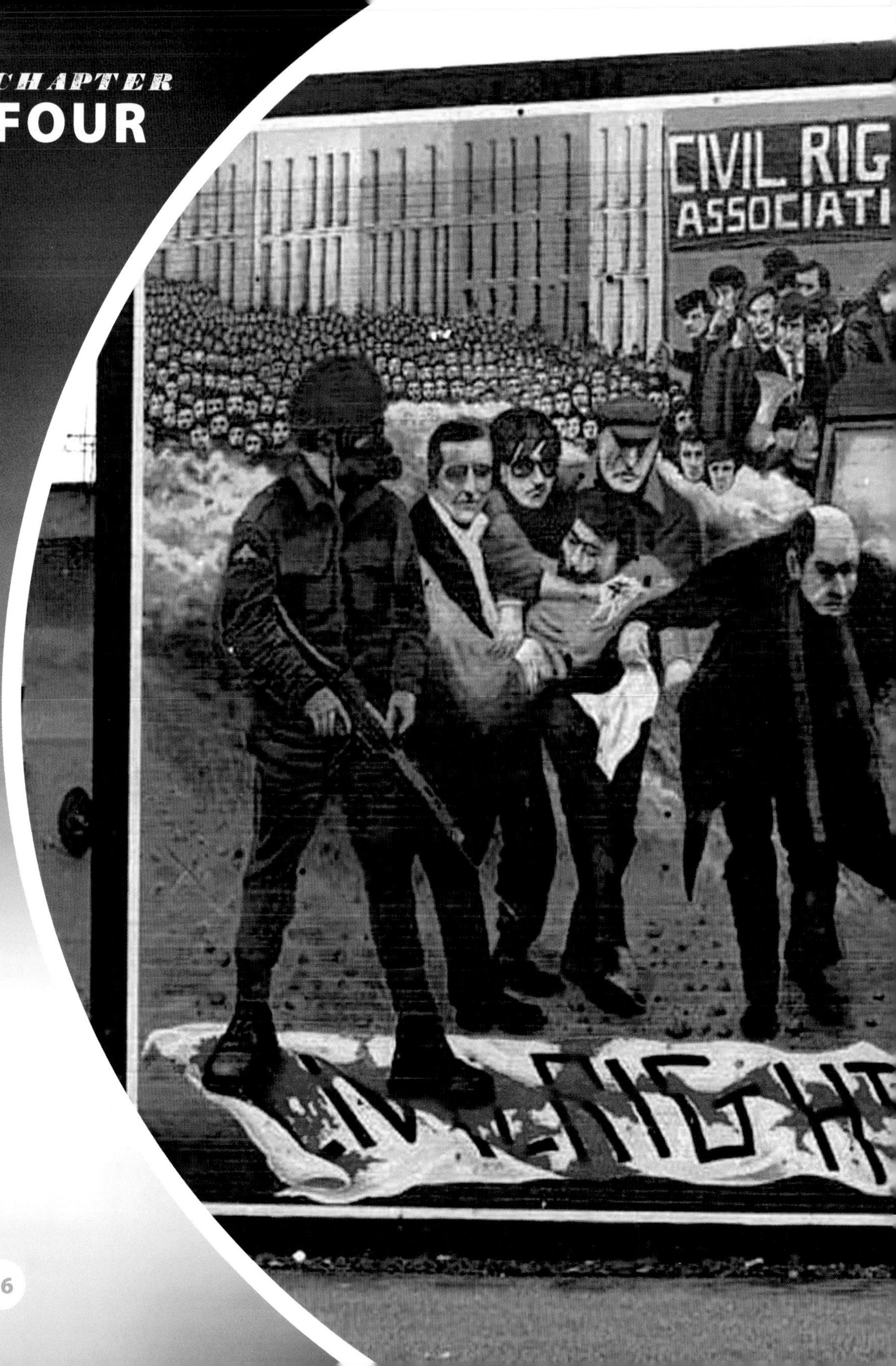

LEGACY OF THE BLOODY SUNDAYS

The IRA became very active after the Bloody Sunday in Northern Ireland. It split into two groups. One group was called the Official IRA (OIRA). The other called itself the Provisional IRA, or the Provos. Both groups wanted freedom from British rule. By 1972 the OIRA stopped using violence. But the Provos still believed violence was necessary. This group was responsible for many riots and bombings across the United Kingdom. It is estimated that the IRA killed more than 1,800 people by 1994. As part of

Murals in Derry, Northern Ireland, depict the events of Bloody Sunday.

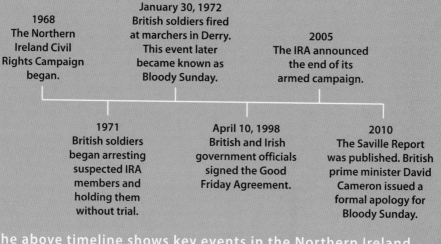

NORTHERN IRELAND CIVIL RIGHTS TIMELINE

1968
The Northern Ireland Civil Rights Campaign began.

January 30, 1972
British soldiers fired at marchers in Derry. This event later became known as Bloody Sunday.

2005
The IRA announced the end of its armed campaign.

1971
British soldiers began arresting suspected IRA members and holding them without trial.

April 10, 1998
British and Irish government officials signed the Good Friday Agreement.

2010
The Saville Report was published. British prime minister David Cameron issued a formal apology for Bloody Sunday.

The above timeline shows key events in the Northern Ireland civil rights movement. What important events led up to Bloody Sunday in Northern Ireland? How did Bloody Sunday affect the Northern Ireland civil rights movement?

the Good Friday Agreement, the IRA disposed of some of its weapons. But the IRA did not officially end its armed campaign until 2005.

A new investigation of Bloody Sunday was ordered in 1998. The end result was the Saville Report. This report was published in 2010. It concluded that the Irish protesters were shot without cause. In that same year, England's prime minister gave a formal apology to Irish citizens.

THE UNITED STATES

Many people in the United States came together to make changes after the Selma Bloody Sunday. President Johnson signed the Voting Rights Act into law in August 1965. This law banned obstacles that kept African Americans from registering to vote. In 1968 the Fair Housing Act was signed into law. This law protected people who were seeking to buy or rent a home. Banks and landlords could not discriminate against people based on the color of their skin.

PERSPECTIVES
CAMERON'S APOLOGY

On June 15, 2010, British prime minister David Cameron formally apologized for Bloody Sunday. Cameron gave his speech in front of members of the British Parliament. His speech was televised across the United Kingdom. He apologized on behalf of the British government. He said, "What happened on Bloody Sunday was both unjustified, and unjustifiable. It was wrong." Relatives of protesters who were killed on Bloody Sunday watched the televised apology. Some cheered. They had waited a long time for this apology.

Today, the fight for civil rights continues. African Americans are jailed at a higher rate than white Americans. They also are more likely to live in poverty than white Americans. Activist groups such as Black Lives Matter fight against this discrimination.

BLACK LIVES MATTER

In February 2012, 17-year-old Trayvon Martin was walking in Sanford, Florida. Sanford was a majority-white neighborhood. Trayvon was a black teenager. Neighborhood resident George Zimmerman thought Trayvon looked suspicious. He shot and killed Trayvon. Zimmerman was found not guilty in a 2013 trial. Black Lives Matter was founded in response to this injustice. Three black women activists formed this group. Black Lives Matter brings attention to police violence against African Americans.

ACTIVISM TODAY

Civil rights groups in the United States and in Northern Ireland gave voice to oppressed people. These groups created a lasting legacy. Activists today continue their work. They hope that with time and persistence, change will come.

STRAIGHT TO THE
SOURCE

Fifty years after Bloody Sunday in Selma, President Barack Obama gave a speech at the Edmund Pettus Bridge. In his speech, he honored civil rights leaders who took part in the attempted march. He said:

> *The Americans who crossed this bridge were not physically imposing. But they gave courage to millions. They held no elected office. But they led a nation. They marched as Americans who had endured hundreds of years of brutal violence, and countless daily indignities—but they didn't seek special treatment, just the equal treatment promised to them almost a century before.*

> Source: Maya Rhodan. "Transcript: Read Full Text of President Barack Obama's Speech in Selma." *Time Magazine*. Time Magazine, March 7, 2015. Web. Accessed July 6, 2018.

What's the Big Idea?

Read this passage closely. What point was Obama trying to make in this speech? How does he describe the legacy of the Selma Bloody Sunday protesters?

FAST FACTS

- In the United States, Bloody Sunday occurred on March 7, 1965. More than 600 African Americans gathered in Selma, Alabama. They planned to march to the state capital. They were protesting obstacles that kept them from voting. Police officers beat protesters with wooden clubs. More than 50 protesters were injured.

- In Northern Ireland, Bloody Sunday occurred on January 30, 1972. Approximately 10,000 protesters gathered in the city of Derry. They were protesting mistreatment by British troops. British soldiers shot 26 people at the protest. Fourteen protesters died.

- Both the American civil rights movement and the Northern Ireland civil rights movement relied on nonviolent protest.

- The Bloody Sunday in Selma received national attention. The US government responded by passing the Voting Rights Act in 1965. This law banned obstacles that kept African Americans from registering to vote.

- The Northern Ireland Conflict came to an end with the signing of the Good Friday Agreement in 1998. British prime minister David Cameron formally apologized for Bloody Sunday on June 15, 2010.

The PRESENCE OF
SEGREGATION IS
THE ABSENCE OF
DEMOCRACY
JIM CROW
MUST GO!
The PRESENCE OF
SEGREGATION IS
THE ABSENCE OF
DEMOCRACY
JIM CROW
MUST GO!

STOP AND
THINK

Dig Deeper

After reading this book, what questions do you still have about civil rights movements? With an adult's help, find a few reliable sources that can help you answer your questions. Write a paragraph about what you learned.

Tell the Tale

Chapter Two of this book talks about the successful march from Selma to Montgomery, Alabama, in 1965. Imagine that you were a part of this march. Write 200 words about your experience.

Surprise Me

Chapter Three discusses the events leading up to the Bloody Sunday event in Northern Ireland. After reading this book, what two or three facts about Northern Ireland's history did you find most surprising? Write a few sentences about each fact. Why did you find each fact surprising?

GLOSSARY

advocate
to support a cause

anthem
a song of praise and pride

boycott
a protest in which people
refuse to support something,
such as a business

discriminate
to mistreat a person or
group based on race or
other differences

integrate
to include people of all races
in a group in an attempt to
give them equal rights and
protection under the law

oppress
to use power and
authority to mistreat a
group of people

segregation
the separation of people
of different races or
ethnic groups through
separate schools and other
public spaces

sit-in
an organized protest in
which activists sit in the seats
or on the floors of businesses
that refuse to serve them

ONLINE RESOURCES

To learn more about the two Bloody Sundays, visit our free resource websites below.

Visit **abdocorelibrary.com** for free Common Core resources for teachers and students, including vetted activities, multimedia, and booklinks, for deeper subject comprehension.

Visit **abdobooklinks.com** for free additional online weblinks for further learning. These links are routinely monitored and updated to provide the most current information available.

LEARN MORE

Harris, Duchess. *Civil Rights Sit-Ins*. Minneapolis, MN: Abdo Publishing, 2018.

Winter, Max. *The Civil Rights Movement*. Minneapolis, MN: Abdo Publishing, 2015.

ABOUT THE AUTHOR

Duchess Harris, JD, PhD
Professor Harris is the chair of the American Studies department at Macalester College and curator of the Duchess Harris Collection of ABDO books. She is the author and coauthor of recently released ABDO books including *Hidden Human Computers: The Black Women of NASA*, *Black Lives Matter*, and *Race and Policing*.

Before working with ABDO, she authored several other books on the topics of race, culture, and American history. She served as an associate editor for *Litigation News*, the American Bar Association Section of Litigation's quarterly flagship publication, and was the first editor in chief of *Law Raza*, an interactive online journal covering race and the law, published at William Mitchell College of Law. She has earned a PhD in American Studies from the University of Minnesota and a JD from William Mitchell College of Law.

INDEX